FOUNDA

JOHN METCALFE'S TESTIMONY

Against Falsity in Worship

JOHN METCALFE

Printed and Published by
John Metcalfe Publishing Trust
Church Road, Tylers Green
Penn, Buckinghamshire

—

Distributed by Trust Representatives
and Agents world-wide

In the Far East

Bethany, Orchard Point P.O. Box 0373
Singapore 9123

—

© John Metcalfe Publishing Trust 1995
All Rights Reserved

—

First Published May 1995

—

ISBN 1 870039 65 3

—

Price 25p

—

JOHN METCALFE'S TESTIMONY

Against Falsity in Worship

WHEN it pleased God to reveal his Son in me, though coming from an old and very substantial family, through whom I had been brought up from my childhood in the best and most exclusive English manner, nevertheless of myself from my youth I had done nothing but live a foolish and wilful life of godlessness in the Merchant Navy, first as an apprentice officer, then as a Junior Officer, but, finally, throwing everything to the winds, taking ship as an Able Seaman on a Tramp to the West Coast of Africa—the so-called White Man's Grave—where, having cast away my own life, I was literally brought back from the jaws of death by the God whom I knew not, who, having saved my life, was to save my soul upon my return to the shores of England. Then I came to know and love him, who without my knowledge had first loved and saved me.

By the revelation of Jesus Christ from the Father in heaven Christ was formed in my heart, and the light of the glory of God in the face of Jesus Christ was commanded to shine into my darkness, a light in which I saw that all my sins and iniquities, besides my inbred sin and nature of interior filth had been transferred entirely to Jesus Christ at the cross, the place of substitutionary atonement before God. The sin transferred, the judgment fallen, both righteousness of God under law and righteousness of God in his own nature, were requited and satisfied in the body and blood of the Saviour who freely—before I was born—took my place as bound in sin and held under wrath. To see it was one thing: to feel it another. I felt the sprinkling of the blood within, and I experienced the witness of cancelled sin in my spirit, and I was joined in union with him who, having done all, was now risen from the dead and ascended on high in light unapproachable, and love inexpressibly beyond all naturally comprehensive dimensions.

But for this cause he appeared unto me, to make me a minister, that I should testify of the things which I had seen, and the things in which he should afterwards appear unto me. Whilst the glory shone within, and my soul was so transported I knew not whether I was in heaven or on earth, the communion between Christ and my spirit being so intimate, so full of divine love, and so uninterrupted, yet, nevertheless, as to outward things, I wept continually —truly my eyes were a fountain of tears—at what I found both in the people who professed to be Christ's and the churches—as they were called—which were supposed to be worshipping God.

Being straightway aware of my calling to the heavenly ministry, immediately I conferred not with flesh and blood. I had an anointing which taught me by witnessing within me, and by this witness I walked. I heard the voice of the Shepherd daily in secret and by that interior whisper my path was clear. I was filled with the Holy Ghost, and trembled for very fear to keep under the felt sense of this testimony. Although I had never read the scriptures before, now I soaked every word, every line, every paragraph, every page of my new-found bible with prayers, supplications and tears day and night, week in and week out, month after month, increasingly each year, without remission. God is witness, I received not my gospel from man, neither by men, but by the revelation of Jesus Christ.

Having gone all over the British Isles testifying of the Saviour, I was called into the Congregational Church, as they call it.

I refused both their colleges and their exams; on the one hand because I saw clearly that here was a pernicious structure and system which did not exist in scripture: nothing but an invention of man to cover up the absence of the work of God in the ministry of the new testament. Besides, on the other hand, like the psalmist, I clearly perceived that I had 'more understanding than all my teachers: for thy testimonies are my meditation', Psa. 119:99. Evidently this was not the case with them, or their system, nor did they seek such a case, for they taught each other, and meditated on nothing but what would enable them to pass the exams which they set one for the other. But to sit under them, or for their exams, was more than I could do, for I had no witness to that, nor was it in the scriptures.

Besides, by walking in the Spirit; by heeding my heavenly Teacher; by standing under the anointing; by avoiding those who taught one another in a false way; I discovered that 'I understand more than the ancients, because I keep thy precepts', Psa. 119:100. Of which precepts, I noted, they betrayed no knowledge whatsoever, and hence it was no wonder that they had no thought of keeping them.

But he who opened my eyes, did cause me to keep them, and this is what led to my understanding. They really hated what they saw in me, and with long faces warned me of my conceit and censoriousness. But I saw through their envy, knowing that their jealousy stemmed from the fact that God had not done to or by them, what they knew full well he had done to and by me, many hundreds of converts bearing witness. Nor could they convince me of conceit, because I knew in my soul that—unlike them, who did everything, and got nowhere—I had done nothing, but it had pleased the LORD to draw me out of deep waters, yea, the very waters of death, that he might get glory by what he had done by himself alone, though it were by such a helpless creature, who neither knew nor could do one thing of himself.

Besides, they could not deny the word of truth nor the Spirit of it which God had put in my heart and mouth, nor could they answer me one of a thousand. Then how should I go to their colleges and tutors who had taught them nothing, or to them, who could give no answer to the things which were plain as daylight to me?

So they were all hoisted on their own petard, and, despite themselves, had to ordain me, as they called it. They had no option, the man stood there healed. They must, what with the Moderator of the Congregational Union (which I refused to join); the Principal of the London Bible College (which I disdained to attend); and this Dr. Martyn Lloyd-Jones, (to whom I gave place by subjection, no, not for an hour, though for years he often and craftily sought out my secret which I had from the Lord, till God brought me under sore and terrible chastisements and afflictions for many, many decades, during which he stood aloof from my sore, rubbing his hands, satisfied at last, that the conceited and critical young upstart had been judged, and 'So would we have it'. But the cause of my affliction was on another basis, that of divine preparation, of which the poor man knew nothing at all).

Still, his very last words to me were a confession after all. He said, 'Your time will come; your time will come.' But I cared nothing for the testimony of this Doctor who had refused to know me in the sore and long soul travail to which he himself was a stranger, and of the causes for which he was ignorant. I thought, How can this great Doctor be spiritual, who despises the man who hath known affliction by the rod of God's wrath? But I had a better testimony than that of the Doctor who repeated 'Your time will come', though he knew it all along. So I replied, 'Oh, I know that Doctor Lloyd-Jones; I know that.' And that was that.

But you will say, This Tract is about Psalms, Hymns, and Spiritual Songs. Oh, well, you know I am always supposed to be praising myself (that is, when I give God all the glory for his work) and you know that I publish all these letters to draw attention to myself (namely, when I receive them to draw attention to the Lord) and you know that I think I am the only one (when I think CHRIST THE SON OF GOD is the only one, and refuse every hireling hypocrite whose false modesty is nothing but a cloak to hide that of which they accuse me. But they cannot speak of what he does by me, for he does nothing by them. If he did, they would rejoice in what he had done by me, for which I give him all the glory, worship, praise, thanksgiving, dominion, power and strength).

As to the Psalms, Hymns, and Songs, I think this preamble to be necessary. For, becoming a Congregational Minister, I had to lead their worship, I was told, and must use their Congregational Hymn Book to do so. However, they liked to tinkle with a toy called 'Golden Bells' during the week. These things my soul abominated. Not only could I never find what was appropriate to the text I had been given, but I discovered that these wretched compositions did not even approximate to the truth. Indeed, the witness within me, by which I walked, and the anointing I was under, wholly rejected such blasphemous human inventions in the place of the sung word of God.

But where was the sung word of God? I knew I could sing no other, much less lead others to do so, but where to turn I knew not. Besides all this, as a minister of the gospel

I could see nothing in the new testament to warrant being the only one to lead in worship, with all these people as mute and unable to take part as if they were in another world. The whole order of this was without scriptural basis: 'How is it then, brethren? when ye come together, *every one hath* a psalm, hath a doctrine, hath a tongue, hath a revelation, hath an interpretation. Let all things be done unto edifying', so saith the minister of God to the assembly. But the hired pastor should do everything, or so all the 'deacons' decreed.

Oh? And who made them deacons? Why, they were elected. But in my bible the *apostolic ministry chose* deacons, the congregation did not elect them. *Timothy* elected deacons. Titus the same. The people were nothing to do with it, save that they were to judge that it was rightly done from the epistles. But nowhere could I read that the church membership chose the overseers, elders, or deacons, by voting. No, nor could I find a 'church membership' either.

Being members of one body was taught: but this, with its overwhelming accompanying truths, they avoided altogether. As to the Brethren, who professed to hold the unity of the Body, I found that a farcical pretence, as I found them a fallen people, in any event on a weak basis. Which of their multitude of divisions was *one* body? Where was the office of minister among them, as Paul, Timothy, and Titus were among the early *ecclesia*? And where were *their* overseers, elders, and deacons, in consequence? What of their error of premillennialism, their heresy of dispensationalism, their apostasy of Arminianism, and their invention of the Mass-like supper exalted over all like the Host, a 'Supper' held between breakfast and lunch on a literal—as opposed to mystical—day that does not exist in scripture, called by them 'Lord's day morning'?

And what of their Hymn Book? Sentimental objectivity, biased and myopic, this was not to sing scripture. It was to invent the ditties of a sect. But who could convict such people, whose view of themselves was that they were the people, and wisdom should die with them. 'Stand thou by me', they cried, 'For I am holier than thou.' Eventually we found in 'Alexander's' a handful of metrical psalms, and in these the souls of the faithful rejoiced as one that findeth great spoil. How our spirit was eased, our conscience set free, to sing such scripture, though found among the rubbish of inane choruses and jangling, shot through with erroneous poison, and sentimental bias. Still, what pearls were scattered abroad in 'Alexander's': Psalm 84; Psalm 100; Psalm 40, and so on.

Nevertheless, where did they come from? However, this question was deferred, for by now, the Congregationalists had had enough. Likewise by now, I saw that Reformation was *impossible* within the Brethren, the denominations or the sects. Indeed, *all* lay in the apostasy, and nothing but a *total* return to a *completely* new work would satisfy Christ's heart, answer to the Spirit's leading, bring forth true worship to the Father, and fulfil all the word of God.

I resigned. I went out into a howling waste wilderness, searching and crying, praying and studying, suffering and groaning, for decades. Now, no man would know me. Lovers and friends stood aloof from my sore. But, though I was under thick darkness in terrible affliction, a tiny, flickering, interior candle led me from book to book in scripture, and doctrine to doctrine in the gospel, over so many arduous and painstaking years of affliction, in all this searching out of the truth as it was in the beginning, and as it was applicable to our own day and circumstance, in the absence of the apostles.

Wholly alone, by now I sung nothing but the Scottish Metrical Psalter. I had quite given up any hope of finding what the apostle meant by 'Hymns and Spiritual Songs', agreeable to 'the word of Christ'. For rather than desecrate worship, blaspheme the gospel of Christ, and quench the Spirit of Truth, I refrained altogether from what I knew by experience was rejected by the Holy Ghost, refused by the Lord Jesus, and offended God and the Father.

Surely I tried: together with the Scottish Psalter, at one time we used the Exclusive Brethren Little Flock Hymn Book—so pathetically limited, so void of the rich range of doctrine and experience in the new testament, so missing in such a vast array not only of the new testament books but of the range of the gospel—then Hart's, then Gadsby, from the Strict Baptists—such noticeable clichés, so much overstressed subjectivity, such weary repetition of the same overworked themes, and total neglect of the range of the truth, and, worse, ascribing to Gethsemane what applies only to Golgotha—after this, immense labour in our first duplicated selection from what seemed the best Hymn

Books, then a far more deeply researched collection from every possible source of Hymn Books, ancient and modern, which we had printed for our use, calling it 'The Nonconformist Hymn Book'. But it was no use.

These were not—at best they were not—anywhere *near* what was sung by the saints and ordained by the apostles in the new testament under the title of Hymns and Spiritual Songs. Worse. We knew—I knew—in the Spirit, and by the truth, that they were offensive—mark that: *offensive*—to God.

Meanwhile, with growth and maturity out of great tribulation and much affliction, it became obvious that for all the noble language of the Scottish Psalter, so akin to the beloved and irreplaceable—Tyndale inspired—Authorized Version, when examined closely—and Father, Son, and Holy Ghost *do* examine closely—the Scottish Psalter was in reality a composition which hid multitudes of errors; some, of the most serious kind.

Iain Murray of the 'Banner of Truth', whom I found to be another of these detached and academic admirers of Reformation History, void of the spirit of reformation, and failing to exhibit the least practical effort to reform the *ecclesia* in terms of the *current* glaring discrepancies between us and the new testament, recommended a different psalter.

This man, one of a group I thought of as Lloyd-Jones puppets, nevertheless for a time greatly admired God's work in laying hold upon so unlikely and unsuited a person as myself, that is, until it came to the point of putting reformation into *practice*, back to the new testament, and especially in *continuing* the Reformation where the reformers left off! But Murray would put us right: we should use the Irish Psalter. Whatever for? We found the last state of the Psalter worse than the first. A pathetic botch-up.

With a sinking heart, and sickening dread, my soul was indeed heavy and oppressed within me when I became aware, after so many decades alone on the books of the new testament, the doctrine of the gospel, the ordinances of the *ecclesia*, the fellowship of the apostles, besides the discipline: now I was shut up to set forth the Psalms in metrical version in truth and righteousness. I knew within me that this would take years of my life, day and night, seven days a week, week after week, twelve months in a year. And so it proved. Indeed, before I could so much as *begin*, I had to learn such things as the principles of rhyme, scan, and other criteria of which then I knew nothing.

Nor had long passed before it dawned upon me that 'the word of Christ' of which 'Hymns and Spiritual Songs' are composed—without which the singing is a foul desecration, the offering of strange fire—would also fall to my lot, no sooner than I entered into the task of composing and re-composing the Psalms. From 1979 through to 1984, without a day's remission, I laboured through this work on the Psalms, latterly addressing the beginning of the Songs and Hymns. From 1984 to 1986, apart from an interval of six weeks in the Far East, the labour was equally intense, lonely, and without remission.

But by the end of this period, that is, from 1979 to 1986 inclusive, the grace and providence of God and the Father, the teaching and leading of the Son, and the inspiration and guidance of the Holy Ghost enabled me to conclude the Psalms, Hymns, and Spiritual Songs. This provided in its entirety for the first time in the English tongue the kind of Psalms, Hymns, and Songs sung in the Hebrew and Greek under Christ and the apostles in the new testament *ecclesia* or assembly. And if it be not so now, who will make me a liar, and make my speech nothing worth?

At last, I myself could sing the very word of Christ, and with a clear and happy conscience worship the LORD in the beauty of holiness, singing unto the Lord a new song, and giving forth the very words of the Spirit in praise to God and the Father. And this I did, and do, as is my custom, from 4 a.m. to 7 a.m. every morning, together with blessing, praise, reading, prayer and intercession day by day.

But even more: I could offer unto my brethren that which the Holy Ghost had given, which was well pleasing to the Son, and which owned the God and Father of our Lord Jesus Christ in that worship which is in Spirit and Truth. For I knew that this was a priceless gift from heaven, no matter what the judgment of the scorner.

I do not believe, in this vile and adulterous generation, that what has been given forth is in the faintest measure appreciated as it ought to be: the gift of Christ to the worshippers of the Father. Largely the profession of Christianity prefers its strange fire and unholy offering, preferring warm fleshly feelings to the reality of God's spiritual presence. To them, seeking a fault, this is all 'I', 'I', and more 'I'. But it lies outside any man's ability, let alone mine. These fallen creatures are both wicked, rebellious, and revolting children, who will not regard the operation of his hands. But the elect regard it. And the saints rejoice therein. And when they do, no language will suit them but that of the Psalms, Hymns, and Spiritual Songs, according to the word of Christ, and given by him to us in our own tongue.

However, 'He that is unjust, let him be unjust still: he that is filthy, let him be filthy still.' 'Whosoever loveth and maketh a lie' let them sing lies still: worse lies, for being cloaked. But *the pure unadulterated word of Christ* is that which alone constitutes the Songs and Hymns of the saints. Now you have it.

Let men say what they will, the Lord has done what he has. If they reject him, he will reject them. If their oil has lasted the journey, they will recognise, rejoice in, and walk by, the holy light cast thereby. If not, they need not be surprised, who neither knew him, nor cared for his things—for now 'every man mindeth his own things'—that they find a shut door at the last, and for all their knocking, too little and too late, the thunder of a voice from the other side of the fast-shut door, 'Depart from me: I never knew you'.

How right and just. For whilst professing to do the opposite, contemptuously they despise the persons, the words, and the works of those whom he sent to them, and by whom he spoke to them. In fact they never knew him, nor those whom he sent, nor cared a fig for his things. His things: such as those Psalms, Hymns, and Spiritual Songs, without which neither he nor his God and Father can be worshipped and praised aright, these being words which the Holy Ghost speaketh. 'For they which worship the Father *must* worship in spirit and in truth.'

Now I give in sequence the gist of the prefaces with which these wondrous works of the Lord were sent forth in order, to the praise of the glory of his grace:

The Singing of the Psalms

To those unused to singing psalms, the psalter presents a daunting prospect. Not only the book itself, but many of the individual psalms, may at first appear so long that it will seem difficult to know how to begin singing.

To assist the beginner, we have given a short working list of suggested portions in the form of an index at the conclusion of the book. Once these are attempted and mastered, so great will be found the blessing that attends the path of obedience in the singing of psalms, that nothing will stop the delighted singer from going on to possess the whole of this wonderful heritage. Soon even such long psalms as eighteen or seventy-eight might be attempted, for a way will be found in which quite naturally they divide into suitable portions.

In congregational worship, when in the meetings of the saints spiritual subjects are brought before the heart of those assembled, then harmonious passages from the psalms will spontaneously spring to mind to support and enhance the worship with singing. Should this be from a longer psalm, experience will soon teach a kind of flexibility whereby the appropriate context is extracted, with perhaps a suitable verse or two from the beginning and end of the psalm to give fuller expression.

No more than a little perseverance in following these simple suggestions will cause the first tentative steps to give place to the sure movements of experience, and this will be found to yield abundant fruitfulness to those who sing to the LORD a new song.

In both private and family worship, nothing can equal the incalculable benefit of singing steadily and consistently through the whole book of the psalms. Places suggest themselves as to where to break off for that morning or evening in the longer psalms—just as when reading the Bible—and it is simplicity itself to resume singing at the same place on the next occasion.

The use of the psalms in congregational, family and private worship has been the practice of the people of God from the beginning. The Lord Jesus sung psalms, and so did the disciples. The apostles of our Lord and Saviour Jesus Christ commended and commanded this practice in the Gentile churches, laying the foundation of obedient worship throughout the Christian dispensation.

The Lord Jesus Christ himself is said to sing psalms in the midst of his brethren, yea, 'In the midst of the church will I sing praise unto thee.' Thus he quotes the psalm from which he sings, and promises by the inward Spirit to accompany the worshippers from the glory throughout the age. But how can this come to pass, if in modern times we on our part allow the singing of these psalms to lapse? But I trust we shall be found among the faithful remnant that continues steadfast to the end, fulfilling the word of God:

'Speaking to yourselves in psalms and hymns and spiritual songs,' Ephesians 5:19;

and 'Admonishing one another in psalms and hymns and spiritual songs,' Colossians 3:16.

For 'If that which ye have heard from the beginning shall remain in you, ye also shall continue in the Son, and in the Father,' I John 2:24.

Finally a word about the great Scottish Psalter, without peer in the gravity and weightiness of its language. Nevertheless it is a fact that, because of its recognised flaws in rhythm and rhyme, and, much more serious, its verbal inaccuracies, several revisions have been attempted over the generations since its first publication.

Yet surely this great work should have been allowed to stand upon its own merit, 'warts and all'. The more so because none of those who have tinkered with it has produced a revision of commensurate weight with the original, and hence their tinkering has made the fault appear far worse, the psalter as a whole having been diminished by the attempt.

The truth is, there is no real alternative but to do the entire work again from the original scriptures. That this is warranted can easily be shown from a list of the graver faults in the Scottish Psalter. I have little desire to print such a catalogue, astonishing as its length and seriousness would appear to many.

Let it suffice, therefore, for me to give but two examples in order to show the necessity for our publishing this new work, THE PSALMS OF THE OLD TESTAMENT.

Firstly, the rendering of the divine names—God, the LORD, The LORD God, and so on—so vital in their significance (cf. Matthew 22:41-46), is totally unreliable in the Scottish Psalter. The divine name has been arbitrarily altered no less than 288 times; added to, so as to make the name quite different, on as many as 122 occasions; and actually omitted altogether some 50 times over. This adds up to a staggering sum of 460 grave errors.

Why have they dared to do this? For no other cause than to make their task of rhyming easier.

However, none of this occurs in our translation, THE PSALMS OF THE OLD TESTAMENT. The rendering of the divine name and names can be relied upon to record just what appears in the Bible itself, so as to give that name its full value on each occasion.

The second and last example I give to demonstrate the necessity for the present work is to be found in the 119th

Psalm. Central to the understanding of this psalm is the ability to distinguish between the seven words around which the fabric of the whole is woven, namely: statutes, judgments, law, commandments, precepts, word(s) and testimonies.

I say, the psalm centres upon the distinction between these seven different forms of divine expression, and the separate experience each one causes in the heart of the psalmist when taught of God. Therefore to translate each of these words correctly in the psalter is essential. Otherwise the fabric of the whole falls to pieces. But here the Scottish Psalter misleads us completely. Not only are the seven essential words frequently altered, but they are altered in such a manner as to mix and confound them together with each other. Thus, for example, as early as the second verse, the word 'testimonies' becomes 'statutes'.

Again, in verse six, 'commandments' becomes 'precepts'. And so on, and on, eventually to make a total of 49 alterations, 1 addition and 5 omissions. And not in some minor or optional matter; for these are errors which confound together the very divine forms of communication without which the psalm would not have been written at all!

And why have they done such a thing, to tamper so with holy writ? Why? To make the task of rhyming easier, rather than continue the immensely difficult labour of fitting the rhyme around the correct word.

Now, to mention from the Scottish Psalter the 460 instances of altering or omitting the divine name, or to refer to the 55 cases of changing the essential wording in Psalm 119, is to cite but two of the many reasons for the writing and publishing of this entirely new and original work. I repeat, I have no desire to list others.

My desire is positive and constructive: that is, to present the psalms in the purest scriptural form possible, so that according to the Spirit and the word of God the singer may 'sing psalms unto him' in the knowledge that what is sung agrees with the psalm in the original in all that is truly essential. By this means, with joyful heart, thankful lips and instructed judgment, we shall be able to fulfil the good word of God,

> 'Teaching and admonishing one another
> in psalms and hymns and spiritual songs,
> singing with grace in your hearts
> to the Lord.'

SPIRITUAL SONGS FROM THE GOSPELS

The SPIRITUAL SONGS FROM THE GOSPELS is the central volume of a threefold work, the first part of which is entitled THE PSALMS OF THE OLD TESTAMENT, and the last, THE HYMNS OF THE NEW TESTAMENT.

The object of this trilogy is to translate the scripture itself into verse for singing, so that the pure word of God becomes the sum and the substance of the song. In this way, those who would 'worship the Father in spirit and in truth' give expression to that worship, in answer to the apostolic commandment:

> 'Let the word of Christ dwell in you richly
> in all wisdom;
> teaching and admonishing one another
> in psalms and hymns and spiritual songs,
> singing with grace in your hearts
> to the Lord.'
>
> *Colossians 3:16*

This verse, Col. 3:16, teaches us the sum of what is to be sung by the Christian, and in the church. They were to sing that, and to sing every part of it, and all were to sing it who would be true and spiritual worshippers. Moreover, what the apostle himself meant by the words 'psalms and hymns and spiritual songs', was what they were to understand by them: a meaning the very opposite to those corruptions and inventions to which men later on should attach the same terms.

What the apostle meant is evident, for he uses these three distinctive titles to describe the singing of the Christian and the church, as arising from one common source, saying:

> 'Let the WORD OF CHRIST dwell in you richly
> in all wisdom;
> teaching and admonishing one another
> IN PSALMS AND HYMNS AND SPIRITUAL SONGS,
> singing with grace in your hearts
> to the Lord.'

Thus the WORD OF CHRIST was the source, and the only source, of the songs and the singing of the early church. That is very far from what has been handed down to us by our predecessors in Christendom, and farther still from the wild and lawless departures from true worship in song that characterise this generation. But that the whole of what the apostle intended might be our portion, and the lot and inheritance of the generations to come, is the object of this trilogy, and the reason for its publication.

The method of writing THE SONGS has followed that adopted in THE PSALMS OF THE OLD TESTAMENT.

The songs are set to verse so that as far as possible the scripture, the whole scripture, and nothing but the scripture, is used in the composition. This will convey to the singer the distinct impression—of what is very nearly true in fact—that the familiar words of the Bible are being sung, and no other.

That is why, regarding the type or form of verse, the simple common metre has been preferred throughout the work. Its very simplicity entails the least demand upon the text to be translated; and hence it is possible to retain the nearest form to the original. The text must of course be set into four lines, each of a predetermined number of syllables; two of those lines must rhyme; but that said, no other demands are made by this, the simplest verse form. Whereas with the fancier and more complicated metre arrangements, the music may be more captivating, the melody more versatile, the tune may be more sophisticated, yet, withal, the price is that the scripture has suffered.

But the method adopted in this work ensures that the scripture will not suffer. Let the tune suffer. What is required is that verse and music must be wholly subservient to fidelity to holy writ. And hence the predominance of the common metre.

Slight changes, due to the disparate nature of the text in the Bible and the fixed, rhyming, verse form, are unavoidable. But these changes have been minimal. There occurs the smallest possible rearrangement, and even less alteration.

This work is not a paraphrase of scripture: it is the scripture. But the scripture set to verse. The method of working has been persistently painstaking: everything, but everything, having been put into subjection to the pure word of God. The result is, THE SONGS are rich in the word of Christ.

In the SPIRITUAL SONGS FROM THE GOSPELS the singer will find a considerable choice of songs from each of the four evangelists. These have been taken systematically, and will appear to be more or less in proportion to the length and content of each gospel.

The exception to this rule will be found in the gospel according to John. Here, a greater number of songs appear. For this, there are two reasons. First, Matthew, Mark and Luke are in any event synoptic gospels, and so bear a marked similarity, in which repetition is inevitable. Yet each of the synoptic gospels has its own distinctiveness, and this has been preserved in the songs chosen. However, by avoiding the repetition of parallel passages, the number of songs in the first three gospels has necessarily been curtailed. Obviously this does not apply to the fourth gospel.

The other reason why, proportionately, more songs appear in John than the synoptic gospels, is due to the length and frequency of the addresses and discourses delivered by the Lord Jesus in the fourth gospel, culminating in the great declaration and prayer of chapters thirteen to seventeen. But how could such words as these be shortened or omitted? If these addresses, and especially that declaration and prayer, do not constitute the word of Christ, and that most richly, then what does?

Here, as throughout the gospels, is found the same 'word of Christ' that is to 'dwell in you richly in all wisdom'. But if by it alone we may 'sing and make melody in our heart to the Lord', then however shall this be done, if the very same words be not translated and composed in song? But that is what has been done in the SPIRITUAL SONGS FROM THE GOSPELS.

One of the chief difficulties in this work has been finding the rule by which to decide what to include and what to exclude from each of the evangelists. Whilst some may find fault with the choice, nevertheless the selection has been made with the greatest care and devotion. Truly every verse, every sentence, nay, every word of each line has been conceived in prayer, formed through petition, born of affliction, accompanied by much crying and tears, and sent forth with continuous supplication. It has been written and rewritten, revised and revised again, time out of number, more than can be remembered.

This has taken—of course it has taken—years to accomplish; and years in which the majority of the hours of each day of the week, throughout each week of the year, year in and year out, has been entirely occupied with this work, and this alone. Nothing, no, not so much as a word, has been knowingly left, if it could have been bettered by more attention and application.

The author and originator of this work has been, in leading, providence and oversight, God and the Father. The arbiter and judge has been the Lord Jesus Christ, for whose adjudication the throne of grace has been incessantly besieged verse by verse, day by day, year by year. And the inspiration of the whole has been the Spirit of truth, that Comforter without whose unction, anointing, leading, guiding, revealing and enlightening, the work would never have been written or accomplished.

As to its faults, shortcomings and imperfections, why, they are all mine; yea, my very own authorship!

In seeking to avoid repetition of parallel passages in the songs, generally the most detailed of any one incident has been chosen to the exclusion of the rest. For example, the Temptation has been taken from Luke. The reasons are obvious: it is the fullest account, it is the one which is most likely to be in chronological order, and its setting in the gospel according to Luke gives the account an unusual distinction. The same rule applies to the one record that has been chosen out of three for the Transfiguration. In the case of the Crucifixion, the similarity between Matthew and Mark allows Matthew to represent Mark also; however, the dissimilarity of the accounts in Luke and John demands that the crucifixion be translated separately from each of these gospels. The same principles apply to the Resurrection.

In fine, THE WORD OF CHRIST, whether in Matthew, Mark, Luke or John, is here set forth in at least a sufficient order, and it is fervently and humbly hoped that this may seem good to every real believer, and to all the true churches of Christ: that, at last, they may lay aside what are at best but the unauthorised and mixed inventions of man, and receive instead the word of God in truth. For this is a matter in which for generations we have all been brought in guilty under this sentence from the lips of the Lord Jesus:

> 'Howbeit in vain do they worship me,
> teaching for doctrines
> the commandments of men.
> For laying aside
> the commandment of God,
> ye hold the tradition of men:
> And he said unto them,
> Full well ye reject
> the commandment of God,
> that ye may keep
> your own tradition.'
>
> *Mark 7:7-9*

That is exactly what has happened, and what now occurs, in divided and denominated Christianity, each division with the book of its own sect, party or persuasion, and not one of them equating with the psalms and hymns and spiritual songs required and commanded by the apostle Paul in the name of Jesus Christ.

The title 'SPIRITUAL SONGS FROM THE GOSPELS' might seem to imply that there are no hymns in the gospels. Or at least, that there are no portions of the gospels really suited to be described as hymns. That is not the case. Certainly no one can say that there are no hymns in the four evangelists. But few would deny that the term Songs—and especially those of so spiritual a nature—is one of the most suitable forms of expression for the very words of the Lord Jesus, and for the wonderful works that he did, when set to verse.

These, then, enshrine the word of Christ, and set forth the work of the Lord in praise, so that by them we may 'Sing unto the LORD a new song,' and answer to the exhortation, 'Sing unto the LORD, O ye saints of his, and give thanks at the remembrance of his holiness.'

Conversely, because of their more doctrinal content, because they concern the church as such, because they are the result of the ascended ministry of the Son of God, the Lord Jesus Christ, the passages translated in metre from the New Testament epistles—from Acts to Revelation—have been termed THE HYMNS OF THE NEW TESTAMENT. But this is not to say that there are no songs in those scriptures. It is to assert that the most suitable generalisation of them, agreeable to the word of Christ sent from the excellent glory, sent by the Holy Ghost, sent by the apostolic ministry, sent, I say, to the church and the churches of the new testament, when set to verse, is found in the title THE HYMNS OF THE NEW TESTAMENT.

And this is the title by which they have been published. And I think none should be offended at this generalisation, seeing that it is agreeable with a spiritual view of holy writ, and answers to a proper order and due arrangement of the apostolic commandment:

> 'Let the word of Christ dwell in you richly
> in all wisdom;
> teaching and admonishing one another
> in psalms and hymns and spiritual songs,
> singing with grace in your hearts
> to the Lord.'

With the publication of the central volume of this trilogy, the SPIRITUAL SONGS FROM THE GOSPELS, the publishers are placing in the hands of ministers of the gospel, of Christians, and of churches, yea, and of the church itself, the ability to sing of JESUS CHRIST, THE SON OF GOD, AND SON OF MAN, from his birth to his ascension, throughout all the pathway of his life on earth, his walk, words and deeds, sorrows, afflictions and persecutions, his witness and his testimony, his wonders and miracles, his discourses and addresses, leading up to his death, into the tomb, through to the resurrection, and even unto the very end as he entered into his glory, according to the scriptures: I say, this work provides the ability to sing of him as it is written and commanded, and to do so with unique faithfulness to the four evangelists. It is holy scripture for singing. It is the word of Christ in a song.

To me, that this has not been done before, that it has not been insisted upon, that there has not been a refusal to put up with its not being done, by ministers, by Christians individually, by congregations as a whole, nay, by the whole church, in each tongue, in each succeeding generation, is a sin.

To use only psalms, and that in such a dishonouring and inferior version, prevented from being purged and corrected because of hallowed tradition, is a feeble and inadequate excuse. A hypocritical begging of the question.

And that this state of affairs has continued unaltered through those ages which have not been without some real visitation and renewing of the work of God, shows how little experimental response to spiritual revivals there has been, and how little the spirit of the Reformation has been retained, much less advanced.

It shows an apathy, an indifference to Christ, an ignoring of at least part of the purpose of the coming of the Spirit of truth sent to glorify Christ. That same cold indifference is our inheritance from the past in the professing church, which, however, fails not to justify itself by garnishing the sepulchres of the Reformers and our forefathers, revering them with statues and pictures, bowing to their writings, republishing them, debating upon the authors, the meanwhile departing consistently from their devout zeal and faithful spirit.

And what has the professing church given us in place of the true PSALMS AND HYMNS AND SPIRITUAL SONGS, required in worship by God and the Father, commanded by the Lord Jesus Christ, indited by the Holy Ghost, and given by precept from the holy apostles?

What?

They have either reduced the psalms to meaningless choral chants, or to a corrupt and inferior metrical version; or in place of the hymns and spiritual songs, which they never attempted to realise or fulfil, they have put a host of pernicious books which they have invented, containing some human compositions from a true spiritual experience, some from none at all, some of sober doctrine, some of wild extravagance, some of sound orthodoxy, some of real heresy, all mixed up together; flesh and spirit, church and world, gospel and law, Adam and Christ, faith and works, and all perpetuated by a kind of blind inevitability, in a *mélange* of confusion, and not one of them remotely resembling what was required and commanded in the beginning.

Is this so important? If divinity is important, if worship is transcendent, if eternity is momentous, it is far more than merely important.

As to the souls of men, generally, how much less are they guided by intellect than emotion? Addresses, arguments, these speak to the mind. But songs, melodies, these fill the emotions. And it is by the latter that the hearts of most are reached. 'Singing and making melody in your heart to the Lord'. Then, 'In psalms and hymns and spiritual songs', and in nothing else; and in the apostle's meaning of the words, and none other. This will safely preserve the people, this will rejoice their souls, this will deliver them out of error, and this will cause them to be indwelt by THE WORD OF CHRIST. 'Let the word of Christ dwell in you richly in all wisdom.'

It was in my mind to weigh in the balances of the sanctuary the perpetual putting of human affection in place of spiritual experience, of carnal invention in place of sound divinity; the putting of words in the Lord's mouth and the taking of words from it; the fleshly perfectionism, the pleasing of man, the lauding of the mass—under whatever euphemism; the error, the downright heresy, not to mention the sheer bad taste, and the childish, infantile repetition: it was in my mind to demonstrate it, I say, from these 'well-known, well-loved hymns', and to give numerous examples and overwhelming proof, and reveal the depth and extent of the poison that lurks undetected and unsuspected in what passes as even the best and most evangelical of the so-called 'hymn-books'.

It was in my mind, yes, but when I actually began to compile the sad catalogue, I found on the one hand such an accumulation of erroneous compositions that 'the world itself could not contain them'; and on the other hand, such a distaste to the miserable task, such a smell of death about it, that I felt glad to sense a liberty to leave the matter to the honest appraisal of the reader, from the true and sober observations that have been made.

Far better, than to wade through a list of the errors of these 'hymn-books' of fallen Christendom, to heed the cry, 'Depart ye, depart ye, touch not the unclean thing.' And again, 'Let us cleanse ourselves from all filthiness of the flesh and of the spirit, perfecting holiness in the fear of God.' Far better, I say, to 'Come out from among them, and be ye separate' to him who hath promised, 'And I will be a Father unto you, and ye shall be my sons and daughters, saith the Lord Almighty.'

And what shall be the effect of such faithful service to the Lord?

Why, the peaceable fruits of righteousness, in the pure worship of God and the Father, by Jesus Christ: 'then believed they his words; they sang his praise.' And what praise is this? Why, 'one of the songs of Zion';

> 'Speaking to yourselves
> in psalms and hymns and spiritual songs,
> singing and making melody in your heart
> to the Lord;
> Giving thanks always for all things
> unto God and the Father
> in the name of our Lord Jesus Christ.'
>
> *Ephesians 5:19-20*

Then will have begun in us, the worshippers, what is said of those in visions of glory:

> 'And they sung as it were a new song
> before the throne,
> and before the four beasts,
> and the elders:
> and no man could learn that song
> but the hundred and forty and four thousand,
> which were redeemed from the earth.'
>
> *Revelation 14:3*

Therefore, let us take up that new song: 'Let the redeemed of the LORD say so, whom he hath redeemed from the hand of the enemy;' 'let them sing praises, yea, sing praises, unto the Lord.' Let them sing with the spirit, even the Spirit of truth; and let them sing with the understanding also, according to the scriptures of truth.

And sing what?

Why, sing PSALMS AND HYMNS AND SPIRITUAL SONGS.

That is, sing the song of Moses, by whom was given the law, which compasses the whole of the old covenant, expressed diversely from Genesis to Malachi, and sung particularly in the Book of Psalms. Sing that, yes, and correctly in our own tongue.

But sing also the song of the Lamb, the song of the Lord Jesus on earth, as set forth exclusively in Matthew, Mark, Luke and John.

And sing the song of the Lamb raised to glory, the Lamb on the throne, as giving THE WORD OF CHRIST richly set forth from Acts to Revelation.

Yes, in truth, that is to be our song, the whole of our song, and our only song: therefore the redeemed of the Lord shall return, and come with singing unto Zion; and everlasting joy shall be upon their head: they shall obtain gladness and joy; and sorrow and mourning shall flee away:

> 'And they sing the song of Moses the servant of God,
> and the song of the Lamb,
> saying,

Great and marvellous are thy works,
Lord God Almighty;
just and true are thy ways,
thou King of saints.
Who shall not fear thee, O Lord,
and glorify thy name?
for thou only art holy:
for all nations shall come and worship before thee;
for thy judgments are made manifest.'

Revelation 15:3-4

THE HYMNS OF THE NEW TESTAMENT

The publication firstly of THE PSALMS OF THE OLD TESTAMENT, followed by the SPIRITUAL SONGS FROM THE GOSPELS, has its conclusion in the present work, THE HYMNS OF THE NEW TESTAMENT. This completes the threefold 'psalms and hymns and spiritual songs', the last volume providing hymns from the book of Acts through to that of Revelation.

In these hymns the very words of the New Testament are set into simple common-metre verse with as little alteration as possible, so that the singer may feel that it is the scripture itself that is being sung.

Although change has been unavoidable, nevertheless it has been executed with the utmost care, using equivalent words faithful to the original, and consistent with text and context. No doctrinal words, no essential truths, no divine names, have been altered or omitted in any case.

This must be very near to what the apostles meant by 'hymns' in the New Testament, and to what was actually sung by the church in the beginning.

What has been handed down to us from the subsequent historical churches, the various denominations, and by modern evangelicalism, is clearly very, very far short of this, even at its best. The plain truth is, we have had nothing like it at all. And the inevitable result has been that in both spirit and truth our singing is impoverished and limited, and has suffered far more than we know in consequence.

This becomes obvious from what has been allowed to evolve at the present time. The renaissance of sacramental hymns, lauding the real presence in the mass, or as they now prefer to call it, the eucharist, speaks for itself. Taken together with the development of the depraved and real evil of 'beat' music, swiftly commercialised as 'Christian group entertainment', with its 'stars' and 'folk-idols', why, this is nothing other than 'the people sat down to eat and drink, and rose up to play,' I Corinthians 10:7.

Had our hymns and songs been what they should have been, the sheer tone of our spiritual singing would have been an insurmountable barrier against all this.

An honest examination of the various hymn-books will reveal the sober truth that none agrees with the order of the New Testament, or of its books, in the arrangement of hymns. Some of the hymn-book sections cut right across both the letter and the spirit of the word of God. Conversely, the range of the doctrine of Christ in its fulness will be looked for in vain in these various compositions.

As to the hymns themselves, the briefest and most charitable examination will bring the swift discovery that many are at total variance with both the doctrine and experience of the new testament, and that they substitute human sentiment for experimental Christianity.

Yet regarding the praise of God, the one and the only question that should concern the real Christian is this: What is a hymn within the apostolic meaning of the word, and what comprises the hymn-book?

The answer is both certain and sure. That alone is a hymn which fully agrees with the doctrine of Christ and of his holy apostles, and which expresses in verse form the very words of scripture. Anything else composed by man is by so much a departure. Consequently the hymn-book, in the sum of those hymns of which it is composed, should answer to the whole range of divinely revealed doctrine and experience, and nothing else.

In a word, the hymn-book must cover the whole New Testament. This is precisely what THE HYMNS OF THE NEW TESTAMENT, together with the SPIRITUAL SONGS FROM THE GOSPELS, has achieved, and achieved for the first time.

Now this—or its equivalent—should have been handed down to us, and nothing else should have been handed down to us. The harm that has been perpetuated from age to age by the repetition of venerated human compositions is incalculable. Conversely, the good that should have accrued from the singing of the word of God would have been beyond measure. Indeed, according to the apostle, not otherwise might 'the word of Christ dwell in you richly in all wisdom', in consequence of which you would be enabled to 'speak to yourselves in psalms and hymns and spiritual songs, singing and making melody in your heart to the Lord.' And without which such speech in melody is utterly impossible.

As to the title 'THE HYMNS OF THE NEW TESTAMENT' being applied to the epistles, I do not say that no spiritual songs occur in this part of the scripture. Just as I cannot say that no hymns occur in the four gospels. But it has seemed appropriate to me to name the present volume in this particular way, as encompassing the hymns of the church in the New Testament, and, if so, the books from Acts to Revelation.

But this is of little importance. What really matters is that we sing the very word of Christ, not the word of sentimental and undisciplined poets; that we hymn the inspired word of God, and not the word of fallible man; that we go back to the holy scripture, and do not follow the harmful and lawless traditions perpetuated by an apostate and fallen Christendom.

It is as true in singing as in all divine service, that nothing can be regarded as acceptable worship but what is wholly agreeable to the word of God. Equally, nothing can really edify the spiritual, except that it conforms to the word of Christ. Moreover, nothing can establish the soul, save that the Spirit of truth witnesses to the conscience in perfect harmony with the holy scriptures.

And, assuredly, to harmonise with such a witness is a wonderful and immeasurable blessing. It is at one and the same time to worship God and the Father, to glorify the Lord Jesus Christ, to honour the Holy Ghost, to conform to the word of God, to obey the gospel, to admonish one another, and to sing with melody in our hearts to the Lord. Only thus can we say,

> 'I will sing with the spirit,
> and I will sing with the understanding also.'
>
> *I Corinthians 14:15*

In view of this, and the performance of the same by faith continually, may the Lord greatly bless both the singer and the singing thereof, for his name's sake and praise. Amen.

> 'And now
> shall mine head be lifted up
> above mine enemies round about me:
> therefore will I offer in his tabernacle
> sacrifices of joy;
> I will sing,
> yea, I will sing praises
> unto the LORD.'
>
> *Psalm 27:6*

JOHN METCALFE

Book Order Form

Please send to the address below:-

		Price	Quantity
A Question for Pope John Paul II		£1.25	......
Of God or Man?		£1.45	......
Noah and the Flood		£1.90	......
Divine Footsteps		£0.95	......
The Red Heifer		£0.75	......
The Wells of Salvation		£1.50	......
The Book of Ruth (Hardback edition)		£4.95	......
Divine Meditations of William Huntington		£2.35	......
Present-Day Conversions of the New Testament Kind		£2.25	......
Saving Faith		£2.25	......
Deliverance from the Law		£1.90	......
The Beatitudes		£1.90	......
Colossians		£0.95	......
Philippians		£1.90	......
Matthew		£0.95	......
Philemon		£1.90	......

Psalms, Hymns & Spiritual Songs (Hardback edition)

The Psalms of the Old Testament		£2.50	......
Spiritual Songs from the Gospels		£2.50	......
The Hymns of the New Testament		£2.50	......

'Apostolic Foundation of the Christian Church' series

Foundations Uncovered	Vol.I	£0.75	......
The Birth of Jesus Christ	Vol.II	£0.95	......
The Messiah (Hardback)	Vol.III	£7.75	......
The Son of God and Seed of David (Hardback)	Vol.IV	£6.95	......
Christ Crucified (Hardback)	Vol.V	£6.95	......
Justification by Faith (Hardback)	Vol.VI	£7.50	......
The Church: What is it? (Hardback)	Vol.VII	£7.75	......

Name and Address (in block capitals)

. . . .

. . . .

. . . .

If money is sent with order please allow for postage. Please address to:- The John Metcalfe Publishing Trust, Church Road, Tylers Green, Penn, Bucks, HP10 8LN.

THE MINISTRY OF THE NEW TESTAMENT

The purpose of this substantial A4 gloss paper magazine is to provide spiritual and experimental ministry with sound doctrine which rightly and prophetically divides the Word of Truth.

Readers of our books will already know the high standards of our publications. They can be confident that these pages will maintain that quality, by giving access to enduring ministry from the past, much of which is derived from sources that are virtually unobtainable today, and publishing a living ministry from the present. Selected articles from the following writers have already been included:

ELI ASHDOWN · ABRAHAM BOOTH · JOHN BRADFORD
JOHN BUNYAN · JOHN BURGON · JOHN CALVIN · DONALD CARGILL
JOHN CENNICK · J.N. DARBY · GEORGE FOX · JOHN FOXE
WILLIAM GADSBY · JOHN GUTHRIE · WILLIAM GUTHRIE
GREY HAZLERIGG · WILLIAM HUNTINGTON · WILLIAM KELLY
JOHN KENNEDY · JOHN KERSHAW · HANSERD KNOLLYS
JAMES LEWIS · MARTIN LUTHER · ROBERT MURRAY MCCHEYNE
JOHN METCALFE · ALEXANDER—SANDY—PEDEN · J.C. PHILPOT
J.K. POPHAM · JAMES RENWICK · J.B. STONEY · HENRY TANNER
ARTHUR TRIGGS · JOHN VINALL · JOHN WARBURTON
JOHN WELWOOD · GEORGE WHITEFIELD · J.A. WYLIE

Price £1.75 *(postage included)*
Issued Spring, Summer, Autumn, Winter.

Magazine Order Form

Name and Address (in block capitals)

. . . .

. . . .

. . . .

Please send me .... current copy/copies of The Ministry of the New Testament.

Please send me .... year/s subscription.

I enclose a cheque/postal order for £ ....

(Price: including postage, U.K. £1.75; Overseas £1.90)
(One year's subscription: Including postage, U.K. £7.00; Overseas £7.60)

Cheques should be made payable to The John Metcalfe Publishing Trust, and for overseas subscribers should be in pounds sterling drawn on a London Bank.

10 or more copies to one address will qualify for a 10% discount

Back numbers from Spring 1986 available.

Please send to The John Metcalfe Publishing Trust, Church Road, Tylers Green, Penn, Buckinghamshire, HP10 8LN.

All Publications of the Trust are subsidised by the Publishers.

Tract Order Form

Please send to the address below:-

                                              Price Quantity

Evangelical Tracts

Title	Price	Quantity
The Two Prayers of Elijah	£0.10	......
Wounded For Our Transgressions	£0.10	......
The Blood of Sprinkling	£0.10	......
The Grace of God That Brings Salvation	£0.10	......
The Name of Jesus	£0.10	......
The Death of the Righteous by A.M.S.	£0.10	......
The Ministry of the New Testament	£0.10	......
Repentance	£0.10	......
Legal Deceivers Exposed	£0.10	......
Unconditional Salvation	£0.10	......
Religious Merchandise	£0.10	......
Comfort	£0.10	......
Peace	£0.10	......
Eternal Life	£0.10	......
The Handwriting of Ordinances	£0.10	......
'Lord, Lord!'	£0.10	......

Name and Address (in block capitals)

. . . .

. . . .

. . . .

If money is sent with order please allow for postage. Please address to:- The John Metcalfe Publishing Trust, Church Road, Tylers Green, Penn, Bucks, HP10 8LN.

Tract Order Form

Please send to the address below:-

Price Quantity

'Tract for the Times' series

The Gospel of God	No.1	£0.25	......
The Strait Gate	No.2	£0.25	......
Eternal Sonship and Taylor Brethren	No.3	£0.25	......
Marks of the New Testament Church	No.4	£0.25	......
The Charismatic Delusion	No.5	£0.25	......
Premillennialism exposed	No.6	£0.25	......
Justification and Peace	No.7	£0.25	......
Faith or presumption?	No.8	£0.25	......
The Elect undeceived	No.9	£0.25	......
Justifying Righteousness	No.10	£0.25	......
Righteousness Imputed	No.11	£0.25	......
The Great Deception	No.12	£0.25	......
A Famine in the Land	No.13	£0.25	......
Blood and Water	No.14	£0.25	......
Women Bishops?	No.15	£0.25	......
The Heavenly Vision	No.16	£0.25	......

Name and Address (in block capitals)

. . . .

. . . .

. . . .

If money is sent with order please allow for postage. Please address to:- The John Metcalfe Publishing Trust, Church Road, Tylers Green, Penn, Bucks, HP10 8LN.

Tract Order Form

Please send to the address below:-

Price Quantity

Ecclesia Tracts

Title	No.	Price	Quantity
The Beginning of the Ecclesia	No.1	£0.10	......
Churches and the Church (J.N.D.)	No.2	£0.10	......
The Ministers of Christ	No.3	£0.10	......
The Inward Witness (G.F.)	No.4	£0.10	......
The Notion of a Clergyman (J.N.D.)	No.5	£0.10	......
The Servant of the Lord (W.H.)	No.6	£0.10	......
One Spirit (W.K.)	No.7	£0.10	......
The Funeral of Arminianism (W.H.)	No.8	£0.10	......
One Body (W.K.)	No.9	£0.10	......
False Churches and True	No.10	£0.10	......
Separation from Evil (J.N.D.)	No.11	£0.10	......
The Remnant (J.B.S.)	No.12	£0.10	......
The Arminian Skeleton (W.H.)	No.13	£0.10	......

Foundation Tracts

Title	No.	Price	Quantity
Female Priests?	No.1	£0.25	......
The Bondage of the Will (Martin Luther)	No.2	£0.25	......
Of the Popish Mass (John Calvin)	No.3	£0.25	......
The Adversary	No.4	£0.25	......
The Advance of Popery (J.C. Philpot)	No.5	£0.25	......
Enemies in the Land	No.6	£0.25	......
An Admonition Concerning Relics (John Calvin)	No.7	£0.25	......
John Metcalfe's Testimony against Falsity in Worship	No.8	£0.25	......

Name and Address (in block capitals)

. . . .

. . . .

. . . .

If money is sent with order please allow for postage. Please address to:- The John Metcalfe Publishing Trust, Church Road, Tylers Green, Penn, Bucks, HP10 8LN.